NOT PERFECT? PERFECT!

ALEXANDRINE HARIG

Alexandrine Harig

NOT PERFECT? PERFECT!

Not Perfect?
PERFECT!

written and illustrated by Alexandrine Harig

From one aspiring perfectionist to another

~AMH

Anyone who knows Pepper knows she likes to be perfect.

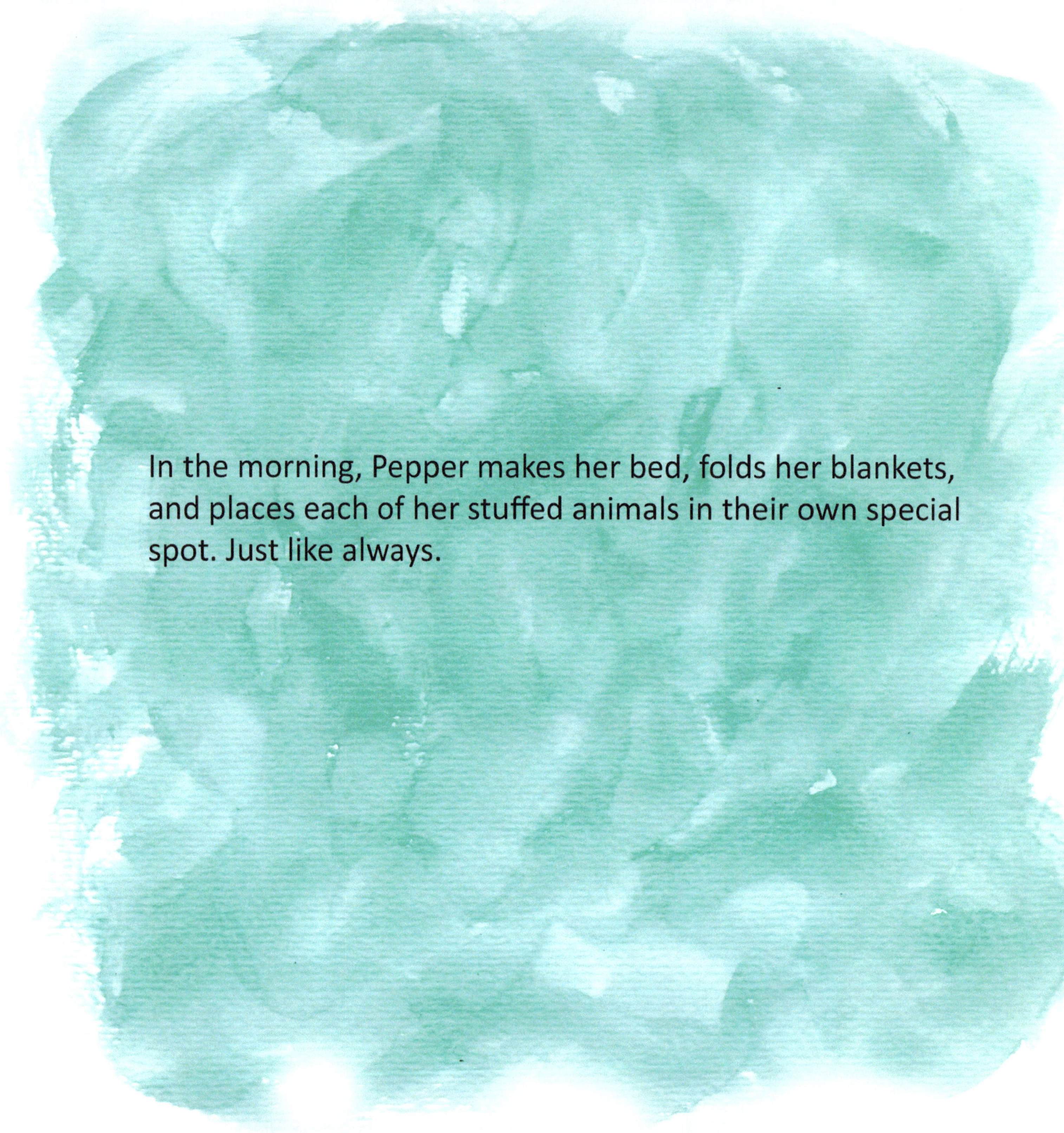

In the morning, Pepper makes her bed, folds her blankets, and places each of her stuffed animals in their own special spot. Just like always.

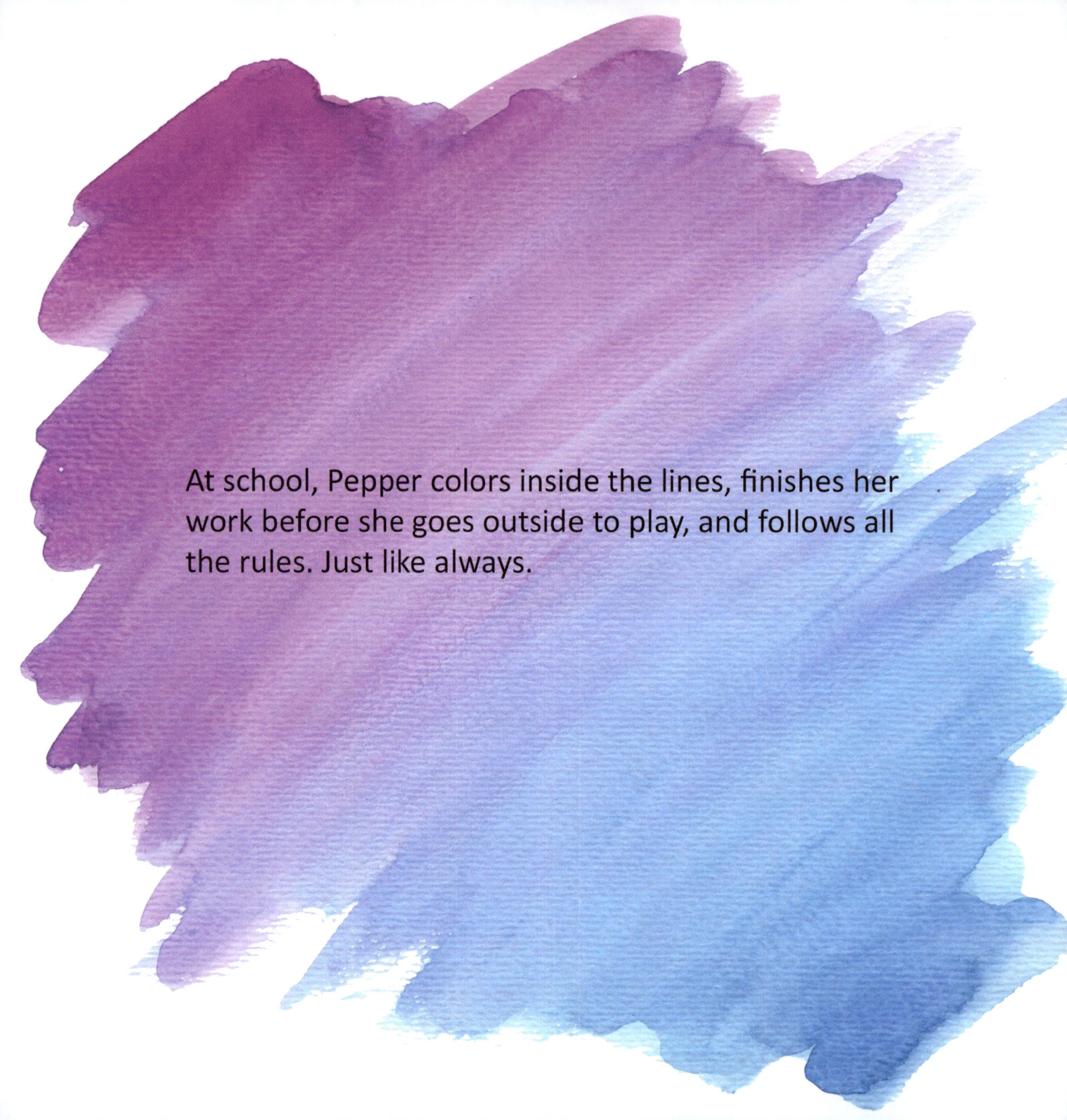

At school, Pepper colors inside the lines, finishes her work before she goes outside to play, and follows all the rules. Just like always.

TO DO:

After school, Pepper remembers it is Recital Day!

Getting ready, Pepper makes sure her hair is neatly combed, held back by her favorite headband, and her outfit is carefully picked out. Just like always.

At the recital, Pepper listens to those who perform before her. Sometimes she notices a small mistake in their playing, and she hopes she will not make a similar error.

Pepper wonders if the other students practice as much as her. She plays through her song in her head perfectly, without mistakes.

Now it is Pepper's turn.

She stands up, announces her song, and takes a seat at
the piano.

She takes a deep breath, and then her fingers are moving.

Up and down the keyboard,
her fingers fly through the song,
even as her thoughts
slow her down.

Pepper wonders if she will find the notes in time.
She tells herself to be perfect, to not mess up.

She reaches the hardest part of the song when
suddenly her pinky finger hits the wrong note. Pepper
inhales sharply and tries to get back on track, but her
thumb lands in the wrong spot too. Before Pepper
knows it, a whole section of her song has been played
entirely wrong.

Pepper moves her hands from the keys and sets
them in her lap.

The last few notes were ugly sounds.
Everyone must know how her
should-be-perfect song is the
very opposite. Pepper doesn't
dare look at the audience and tries to
decide what to do.

Should she let herself cry and THROW a tantrum?

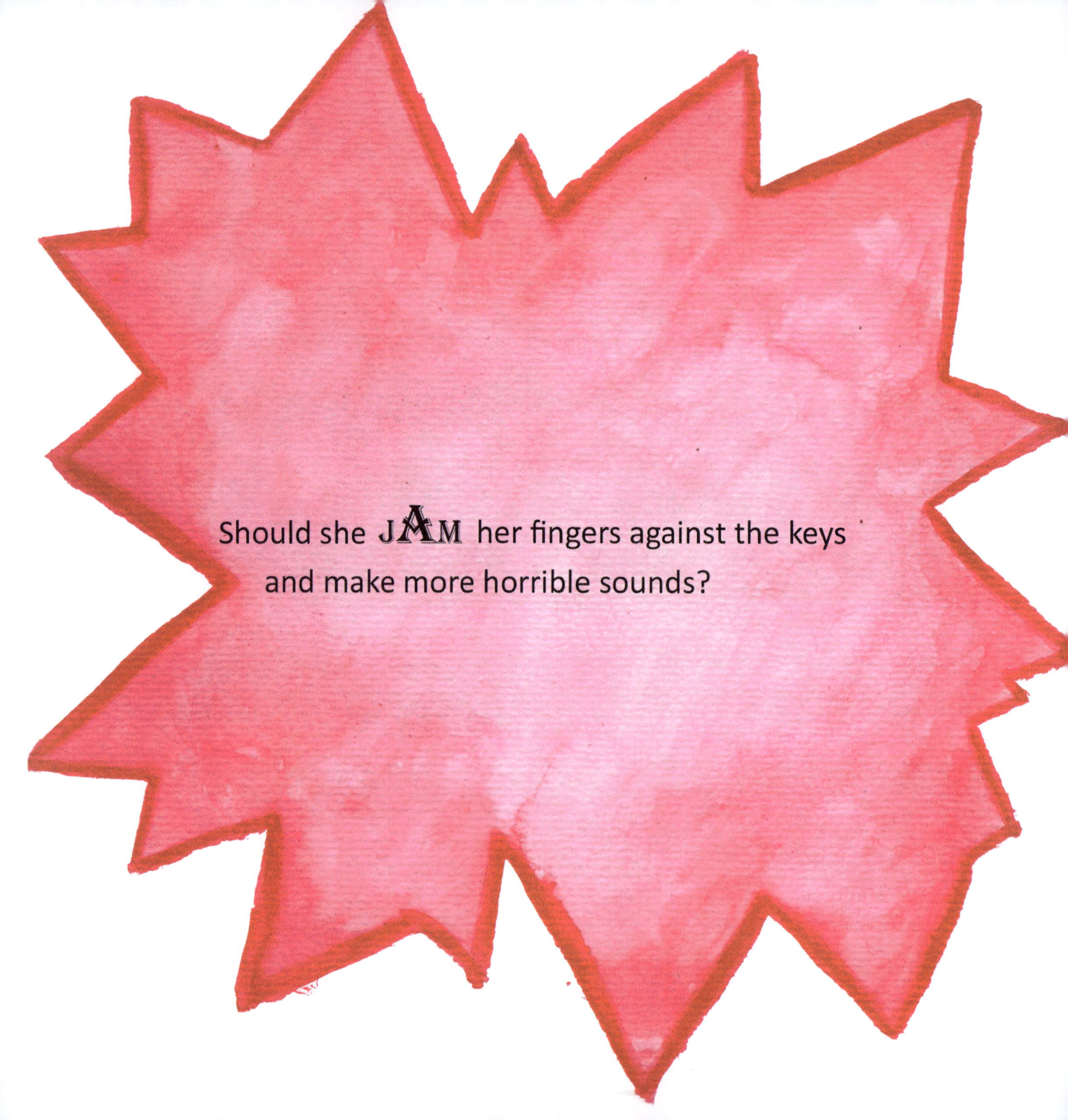

Should she JAM her fingers against the keys
and make more horrible sounds?

Should she KICK at the piano and SCREAM
as loudly as possible?

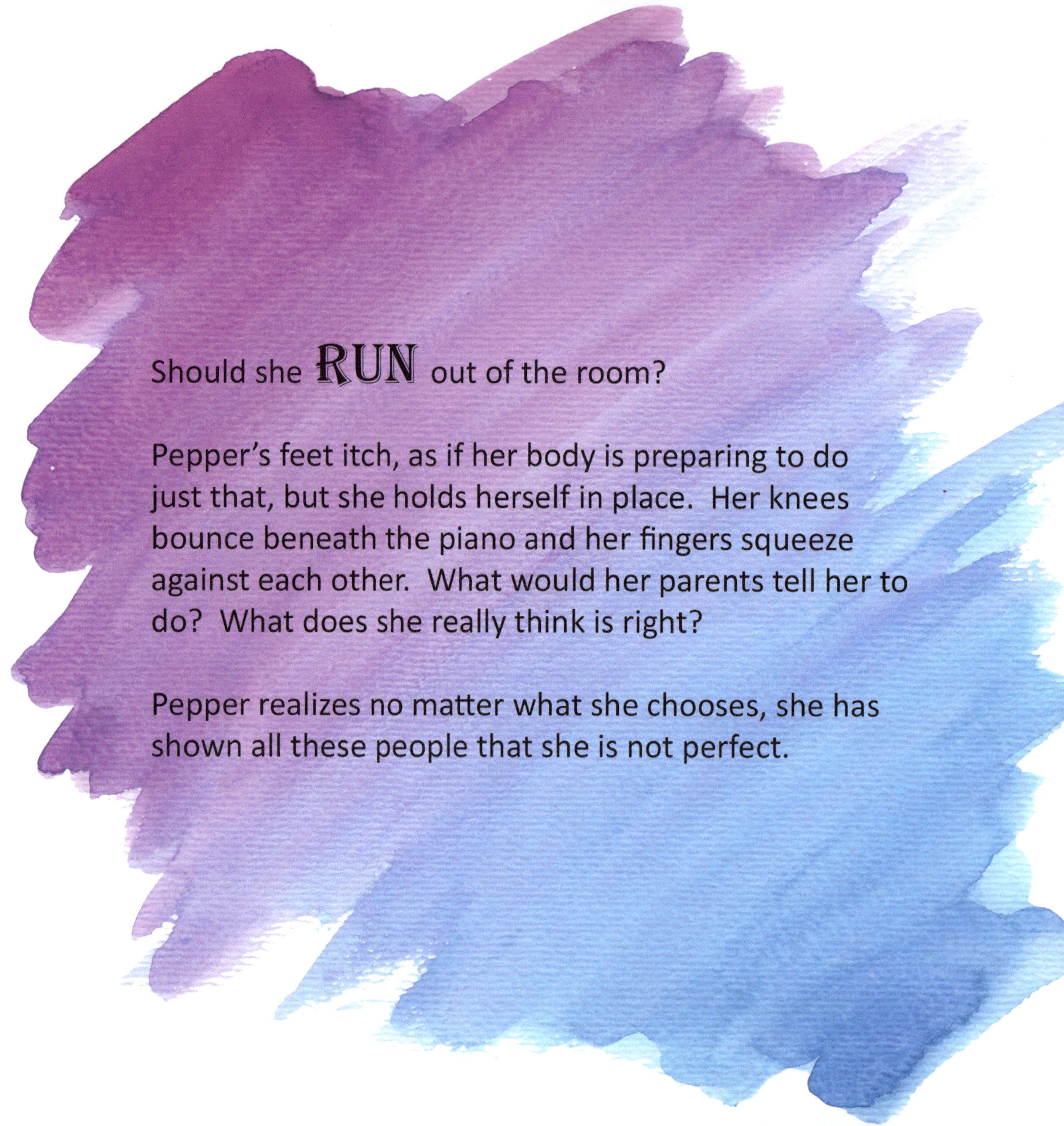

Should she **RUN** out of the room?

Pepper's feet itch, as if her body is preparing to do just that, but she holds herself in place. Her knees bounce beneath the piano and her fingers squeeze against each other. What would her parents tell her to do? What does she really think is right?

Pepper realizes no matter what she chooses, she has shown all these people that she is not perfect.

But, Pepper still wants to play her piece. She worked
so hard on it!

Pepper makes her decision and looks at the audience.

Pepper clears her throat.

"I'm –" the word is too quiet to be heard by the
whole room. She tries again. "I'm going to start over."

Pepper begins a second time. Now that she has already made a mistake, she finds it more fun.

This time as she plays, her thoughts do not scare her about making mistakes. She already made mistakes, and she was fine! Now she is just playing to play.

Pepper finishes the piece with a few more mistakes - still not perfect, but beautiful all the same.

Pepper smiles.

There is a warm, fuzzy feeling in her stomach. The music seems to have replaced the jitters with a feeling of sunshine, like lemonade on a hot summer day. She feels like she could leap for joy or run a marathon.

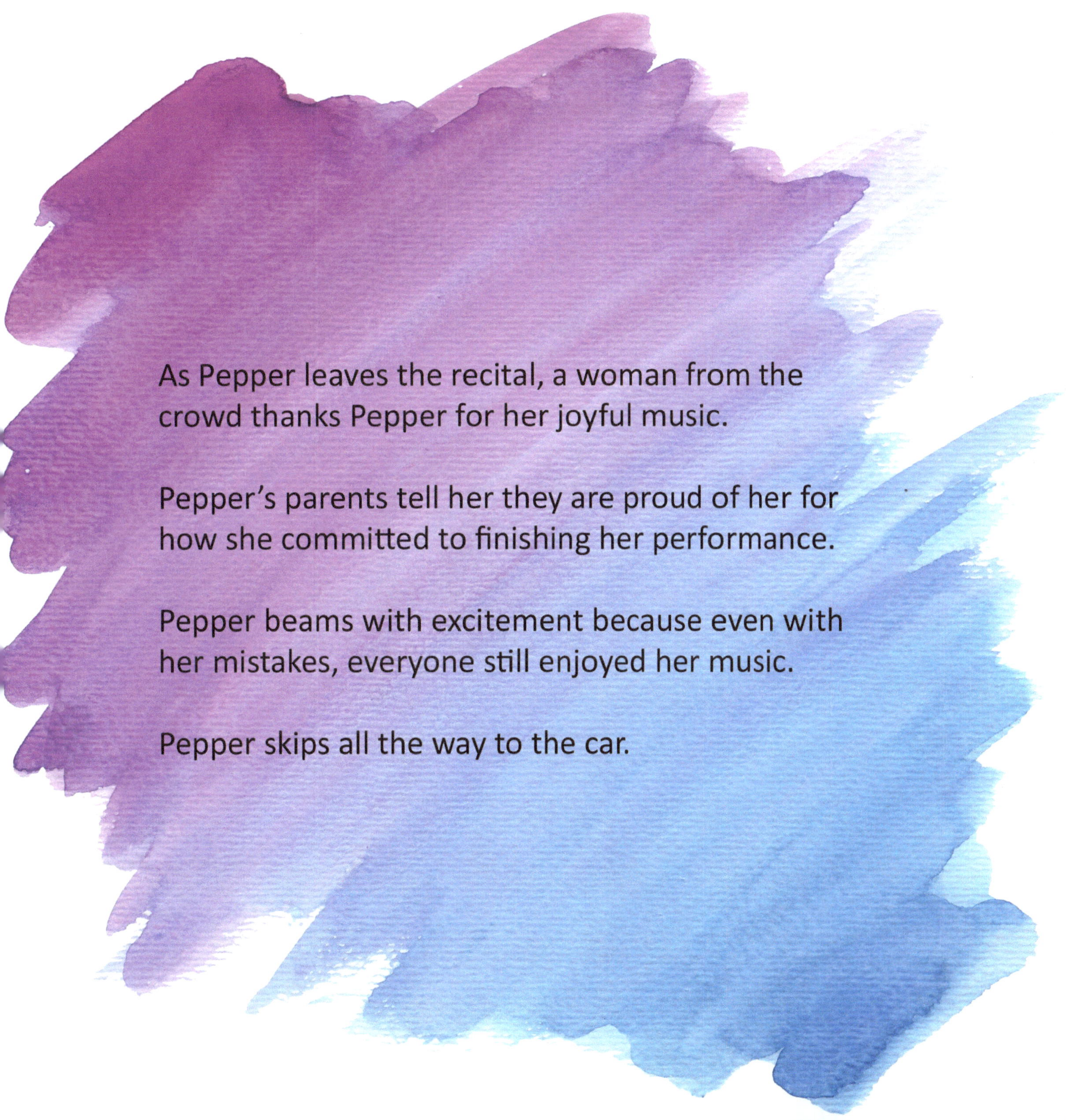
As Pepper leaves the recital, a woman from the
crowd thanks Pepper for her joyful music.

Pepper's parents tell her they are proud of her for
how she committed to finishing her performance.

Pepper beams with excitement because even with
her mistakes, everyone still enjoyed her music.

Pepper skips all the way to the car.

Not perfect? Perfect! Neither is Pepper.

TO DO:

Acknowledgements

A huge thank you to my parents for their help and support throughout this process. A special thanks to Erika Lynne Jones and Jamie Robyn Wood for their time, effort, and feedback. Without their help and expertise this book would not be where it is now. They helped me to think about my story on a deeper level and improve both my writing and my illustrations. With much gratitude, I want to thank author Lindsey Leavitt-Brown for getting me started and being a source of inspiration. And finally, thank you to James Brown and Rudy Shaffer from Water for Life Charity for supporting me in my service journey and inspiring me to continue doing more.